STAR WARS®
EPISODE I

BATTLES TO COLOUR

written by Kerry Milliron
illustrated by David Boller

SCHOLASTIC

LUCAS BOOKS

© 1999 Lucasfilm Ltd. & TM. All rights reserved. Used under authorization.

ISBN: 0 439 01416 6
www.starwars.com

First published in the United States of America by Random House Inc., New York, 1999.
Printed in the United Kingdom 10 9 8 7 6 5 4 3 2 1

Trade Federation ships surround the
peaceful planet of Naboo.

The Jedi have come to negotiate for peace.

"Poison gas!"

Negotiations are over!

The swamps of Naboo

Qui-Gon saves
Jar Jar Binks from
being squashed
like a fly.

Obi-Wan's lightsaber

Droids attack!

Qui-Gon
deflects their blasts…

Trouble is brewing on Naboo.

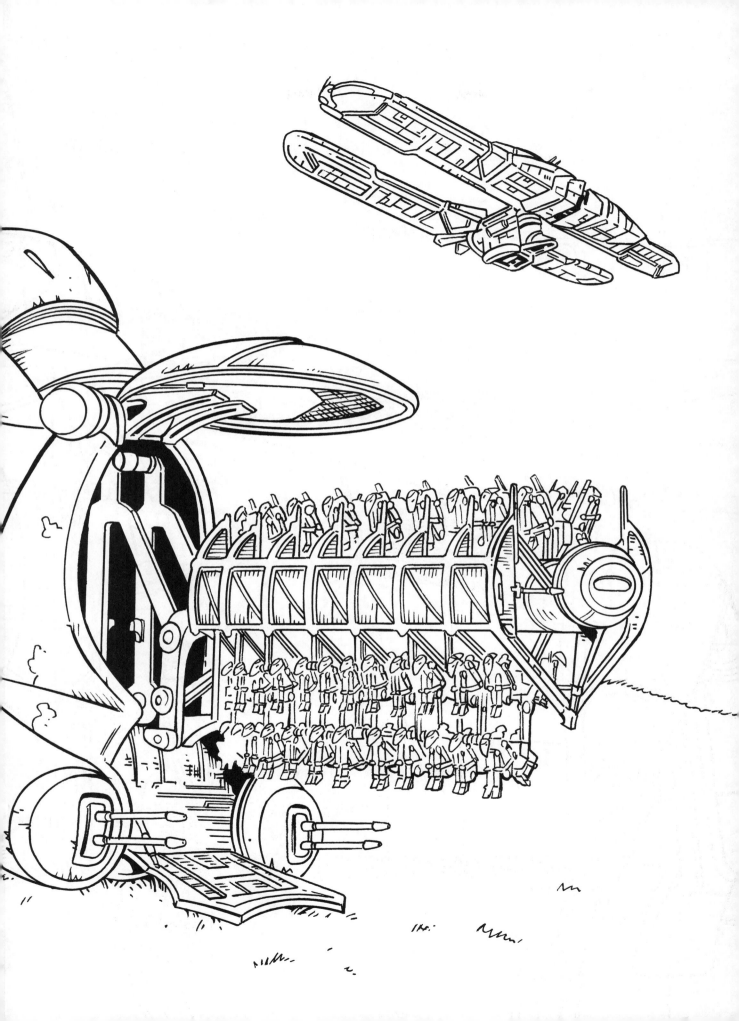

Queen Amidala is a prisoner in her own castle!

"You are under arrest," says the battle droid.

Jedi Knights don't
like being arrested.

Escape from Naboo!

...almost.

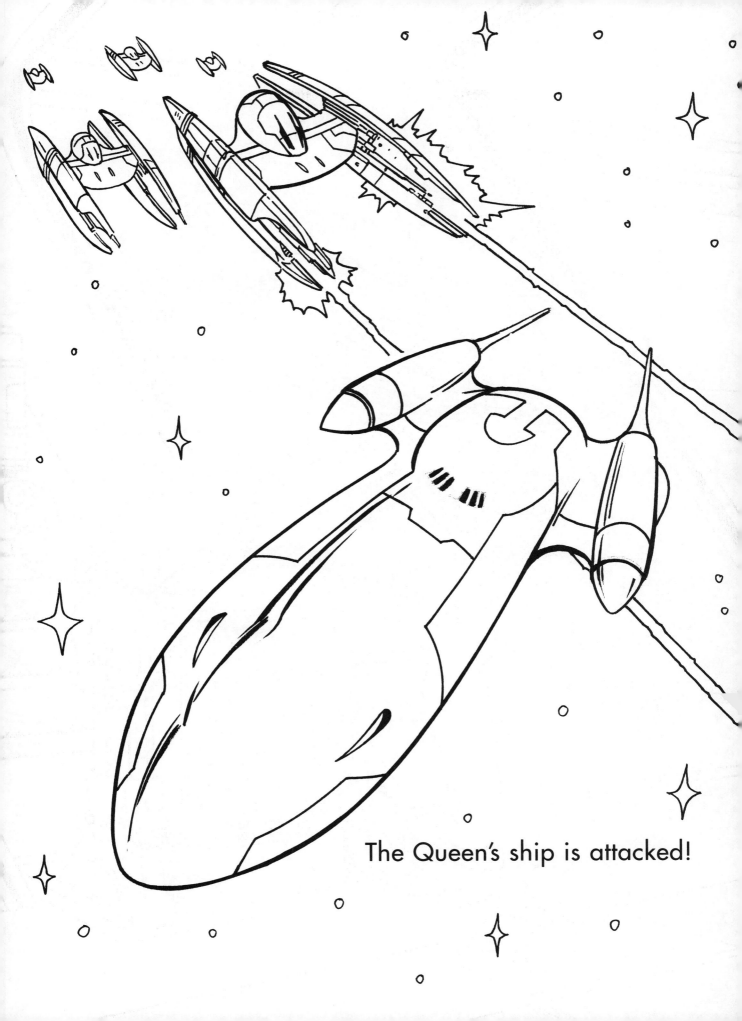

The Queen's ship is attacked!

Who is that little droid?

It's R2-D2. He has saved the day!

The Gungans have a great army...

...and Jar Jar
has been made a general.

"Oie, bantha poo-doo!"

The droid army is very fierce!

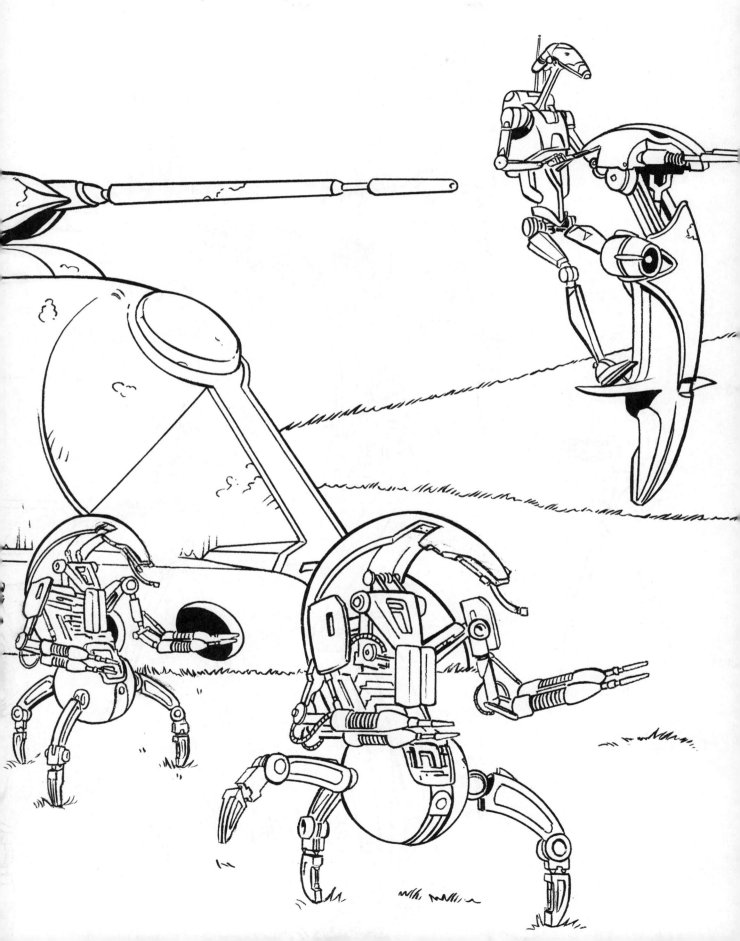

Battle droids are scary.

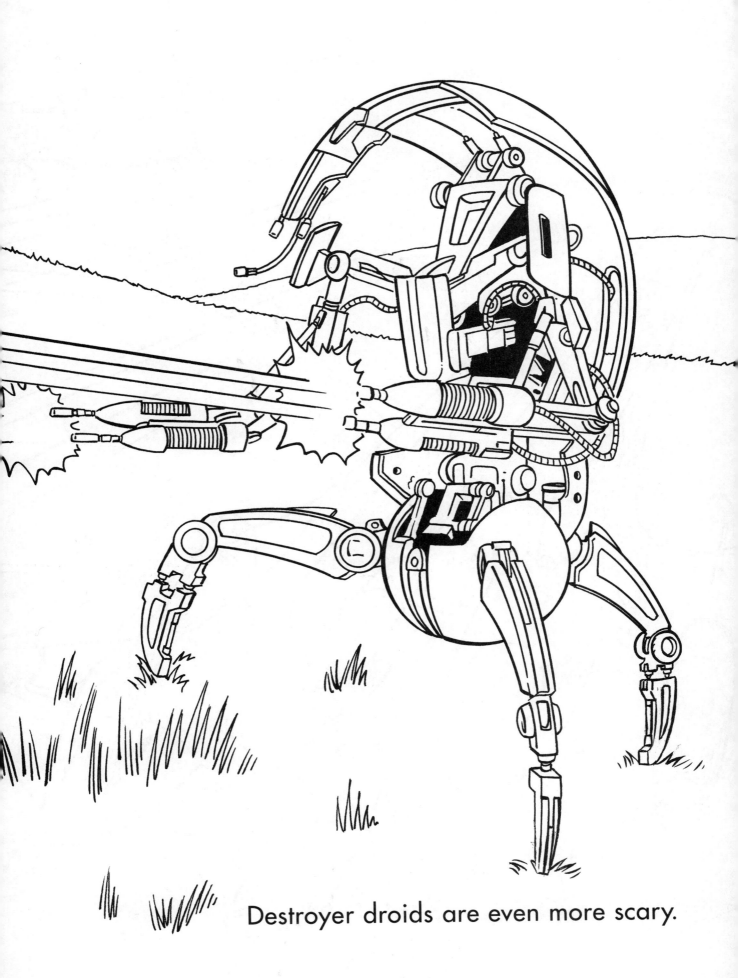

Destroyer droids are even more scary.

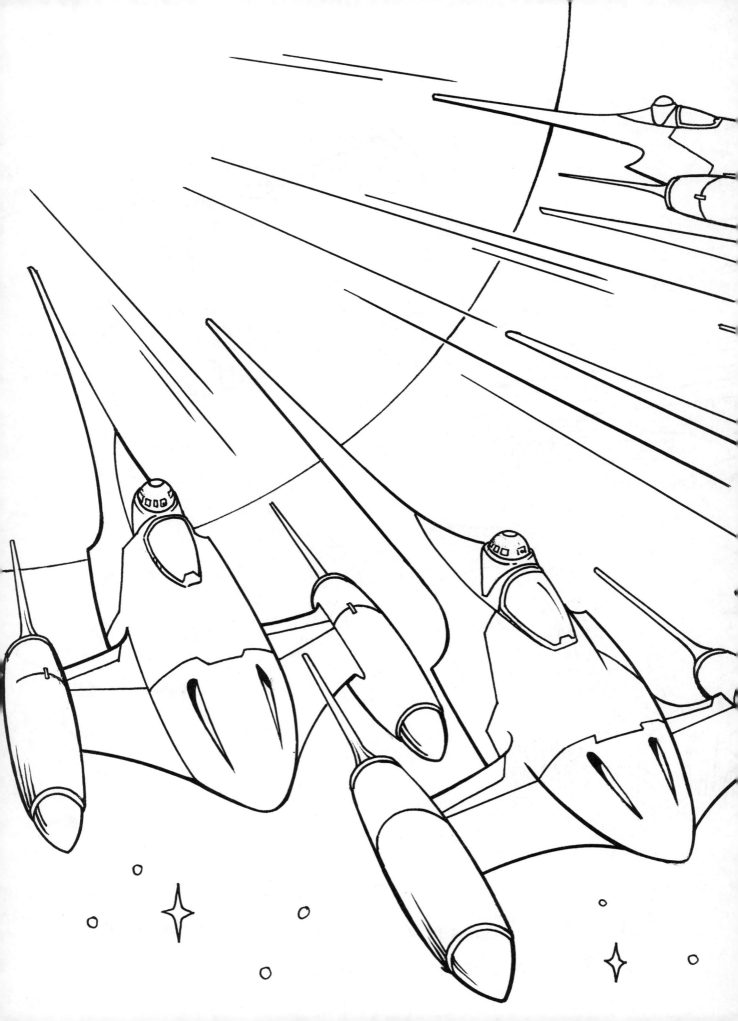

Royal Security Forces of Naboo

The Trade Federation has droids
that change into fighter ships.

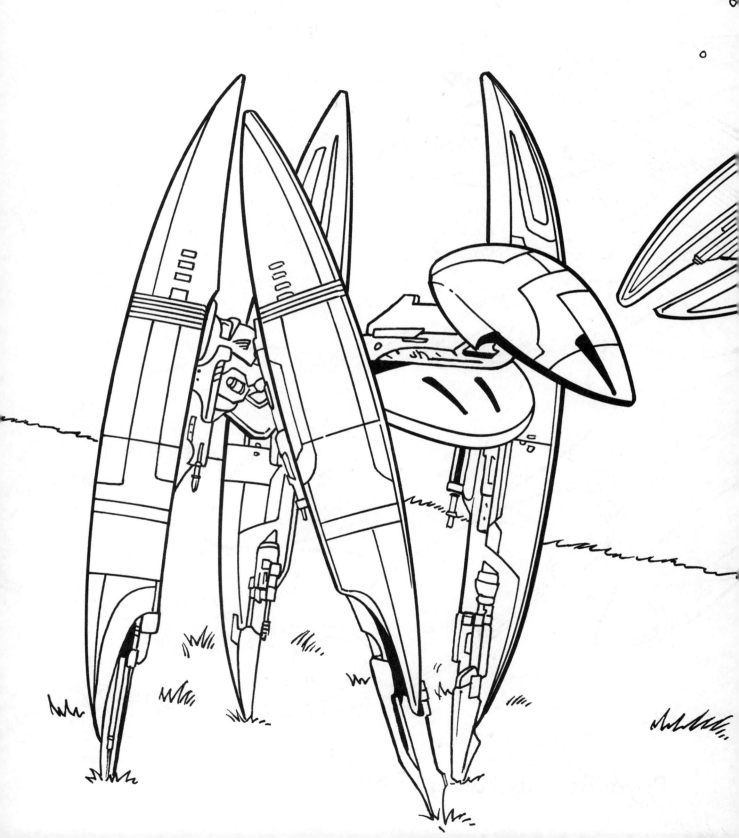

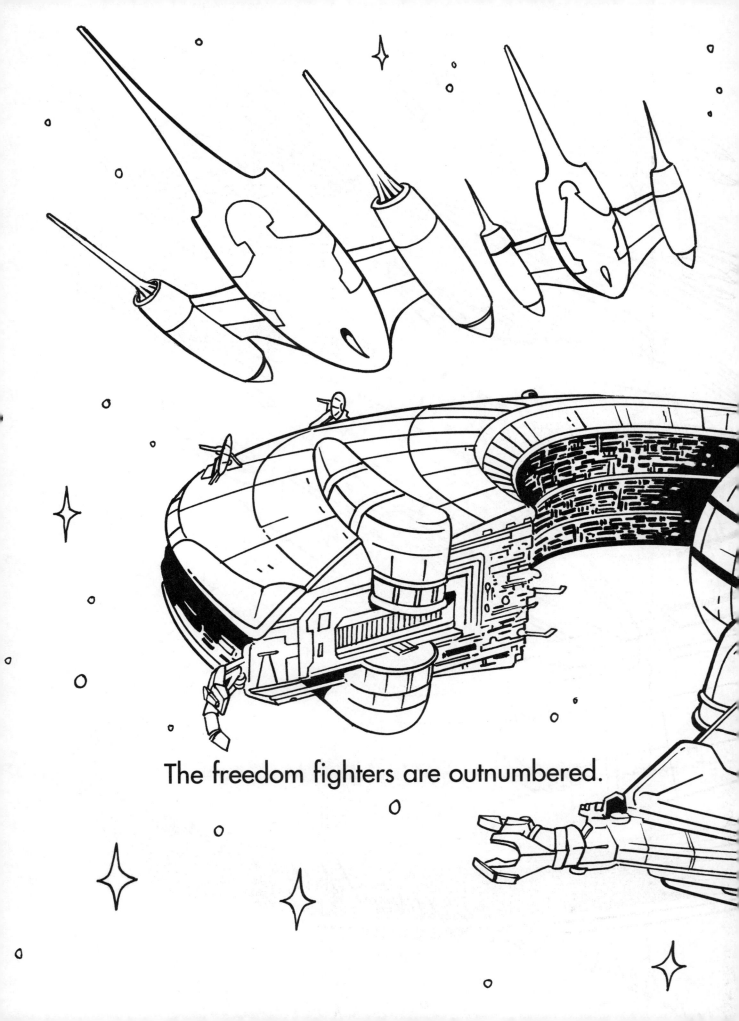

The freedom fighters are outnumbered.

Can Anakin help?

Oops!

The land battle begins.

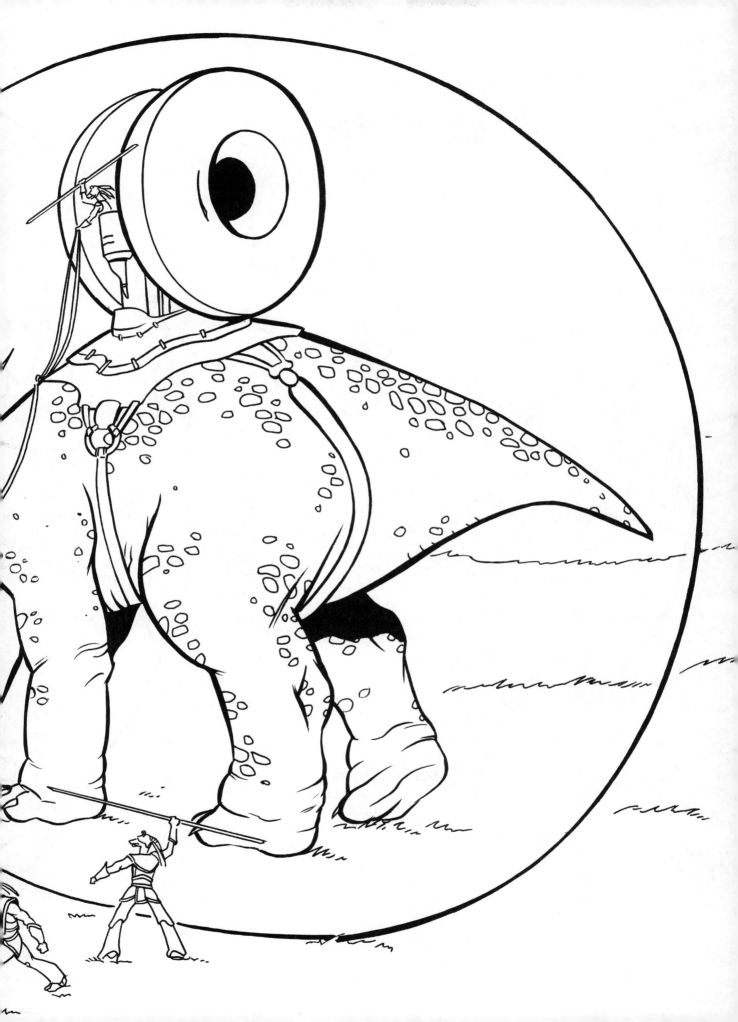

Gungans fight with spears...

Kaadu can travel
on land and in water.

Fambaas carry
huge Gungan
shield generators.

Sometimes the Force is with Jar Jar.

Sometimes Jar Jar is just lucky.

Hold on, Jar Jar!

Anakin and R2 fly into the space battle...

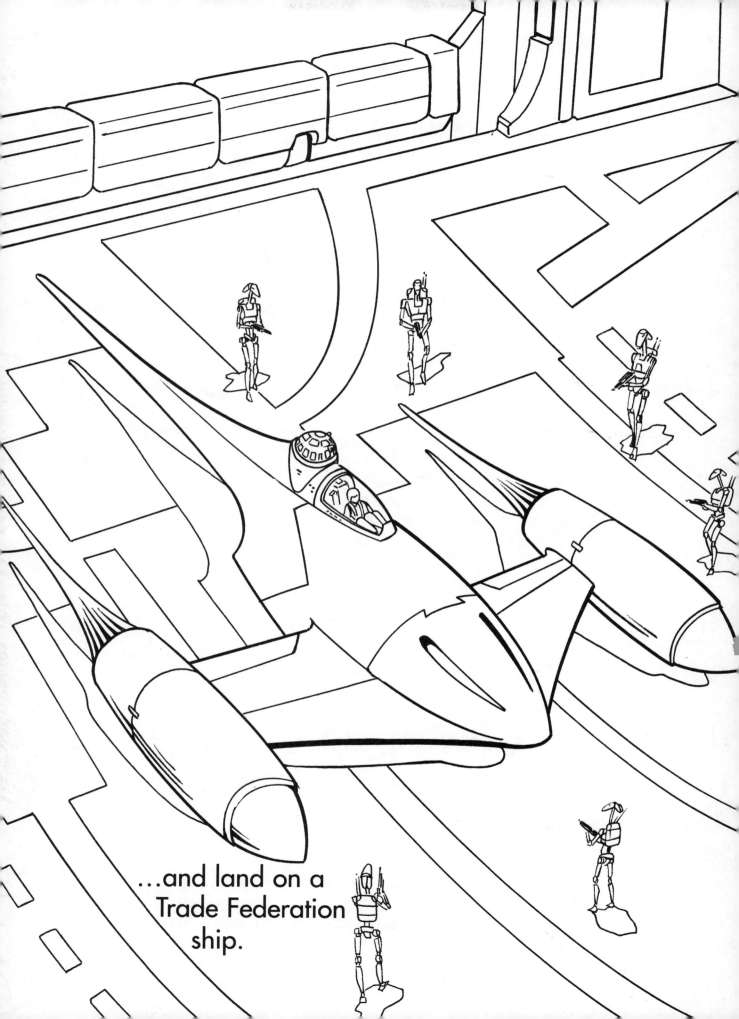

...and land on a
Trade Federation
ship.

Naboo starfighters are fast...

...but the Trade Federation
has bigger guns.

The battle is fierce.

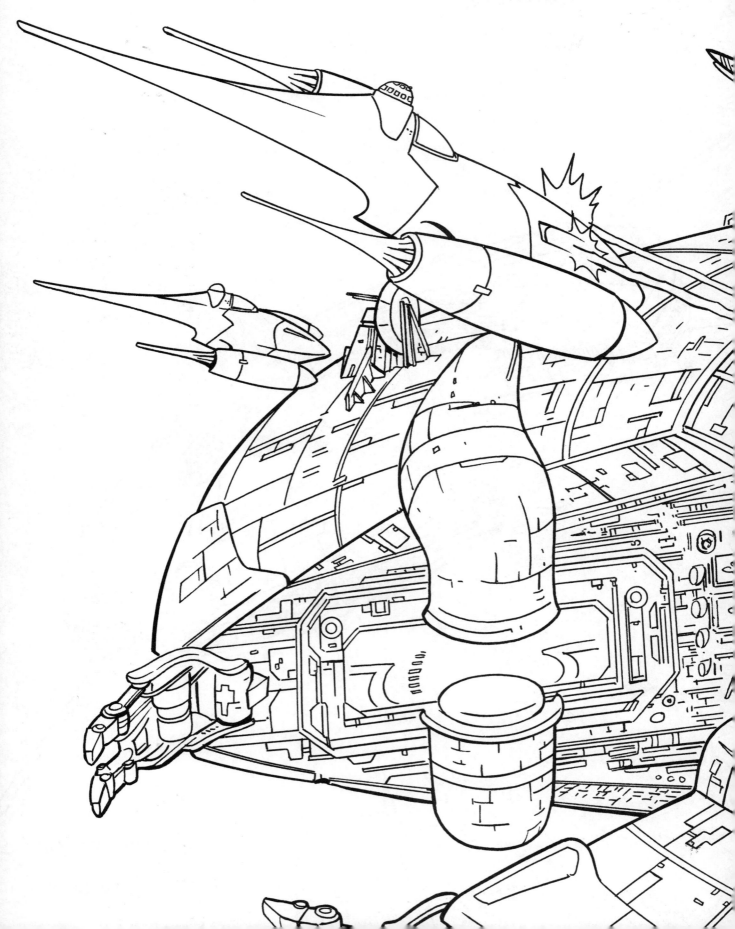

Anakin clears the deck.

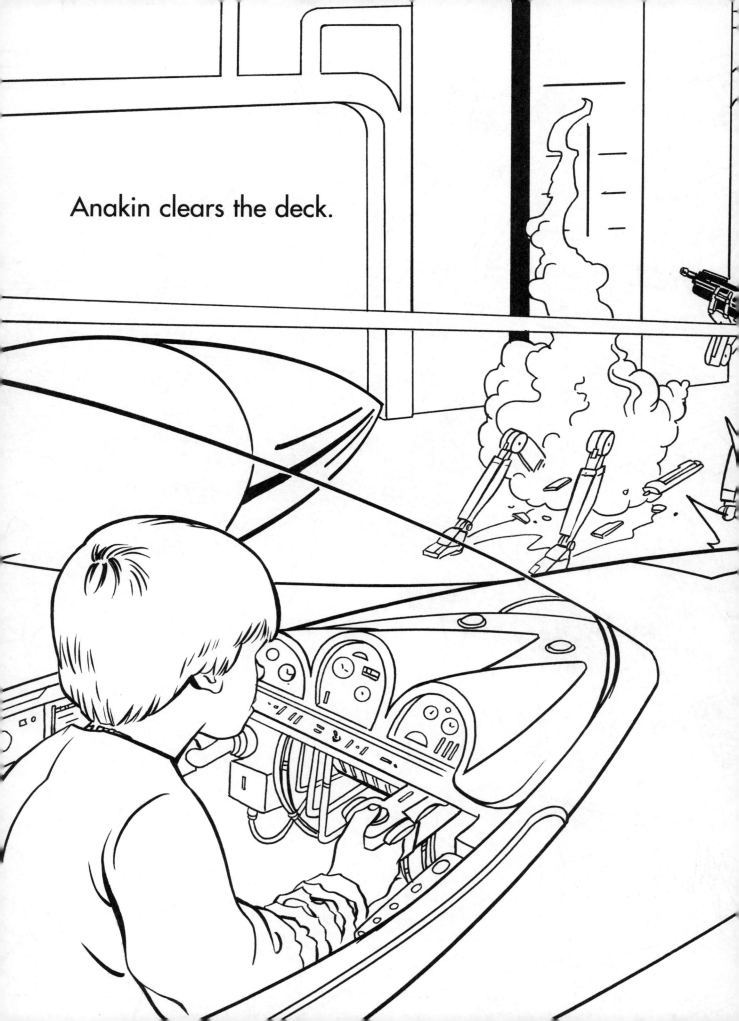

This is better than Podracing!

"I'm not going to get into trouble, am I?"

Padmé
and friends try
to recapture Theed.

The Jedi have a dangerous enemy.

Darth Maul draws his power
from the dark side of the Force.

Can the Sith Lord be beaten?

Sometimes you have
to make your own way.

Is Padmé really the Queen in disguise?

Padmé
has other
surprises,
too.

"This is the end of your occupation."

Time to celebrate!